Loss,

Life &

Love

thru my experiences

Lee Publishing Group
Atlanta, Georgia

ISBN: 978-069-2887141

ACKNOWLEDGEMENTS

I wish to acknowledge all my family and friends that believed in me. Each and every one played a valuable role in my accomplishing this goal. A special shout out goes to my uncle, Donnie. (Robert Lee Jones) May he rest in eternal peace. He left us far too soon. He gave me his permission to use Richard's picture in this publication. He knew the bond we shared.

To my aunt, Priscilla Price, who encouraged my creativity from middle school to adulthood. She kept every article, short story and art project that I ever did. Love you to life.

To my friend, George Dorsey, Jr. who is always challenging and pushing me. I told him about my desire to be an author and spoken word artist. He challenged me to get on stage at Apache Café in Atlanta, Georgia. Thank you for that George because it developed my confidence to share my gift to a large audience.

To my parents, Oscar A. and Edith J. Hunter. You are my creators and from you my creativity was born. I truly thank you. I have learned from each one of you separately and collectively. If there were no you, there would be no me.

Loss

Life

Love

M   Is for all the mistakes

I   Is for the influences others make

C   Is for what couldn't be done

H   Is for the hell but the victories won

E   Is for the effort to make things right

L   Is for all the lies that were told to me

L   Is for the love I give so freely

E   Is for the everlasting love I hope to continue to share

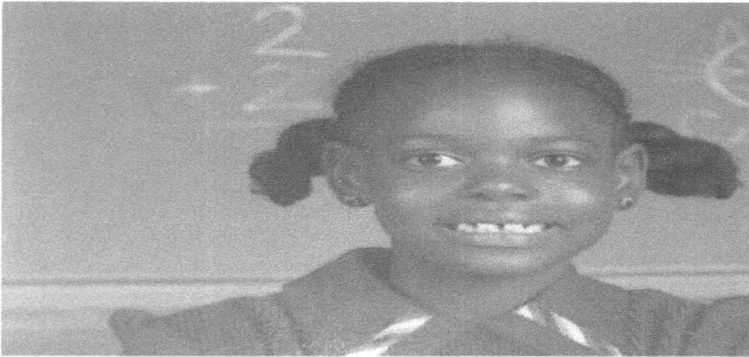

Pretending

Adele's song, "*Hello*" totally speaks to me
Bringing you back up from my memory
Along with the sadness and pain of yesterday
She says it all
What more can I say?
I guess I could tell you my love never ended
Even though for the most part I pretended
Pretended that my heart didn't break
Knowing that day you were getting married for
Heaven's sake
Pretending that it all didn't matter
Pretending that my world didn't shatter
Pretending that you never crossed my mind
Trying to stay in the current time
Not wanting to get lost in our past
Trying to make excuses for why it didn't last
But, that was so long ago
I won't continue to torture myself
No more, pretending.

Untiled

As the wind blows, I think of you
And all the wonderful things you do
Since you've been gone so far away
I realize how much I need to say
I miss you and want you here
I'm making wishes for you to appear
So Magic Genie hear my cry
Please bring back my favorite guy

Untitled

When the sun rises out from the clouds
Listen for my voice for I'll shout out loud
I'm at peace here and finally belong
I wish to hear from you a happy song
Don't be sad for I never could be
I want joy and most of all for you to remember me

For my Cousin Richard

21 years we had you as a family
Watching you grow discussing how your future would
be
Then that day the phone rang
I never knew anguish news like that could bring
Someone said, "Richard's gone" and my knees went
weak
I fell to the floor and began to weep
Not my Richard, my little cousin we sheltered from the
Boston streets
How could this happen he was safe and away at
college?
This must be a mistake
Unfortunately, it wasn't. God knew the soul to take
My angel Richard loved to play basketball
That boy grew to be over six feet tall
When they said, "he collapsed on the court",
I said at least he was playing his favorite sport
But the pain of not having him with me was a lot to
bear
Sometimes I feel life just isn't fair
My angel, my Richard was a superstar chasing his
dreams
Now he's our guardian angel flexing his wings
So many questions and not enough answers but he's
resting now
We'll meet again, I don't know when and I don't know
how
One thing's for sure, it'll be a party that day

Because I will be made whole again, I pray
Each time a family member dies, it takes a piece of
me
Even though I know they live on in eternity
I have the fondest moments stored in my memory
bank
And for that, I am grateful
It's still hard not to want to turn back the hands of time
Go to that day and press rewind
So, I can tell Richard, "No cuz you shouldn't practice
today"
Even though I know exactly what he'd say
"Nah man, coach says no practice, I can't play"
Then I could only say, "Alright, do you, big head. I
love you."
He would say, "yeah yeah I love you too"

Today I Cried

Just the other day
I thought I heard you call my name
I turned around slowly but to my shame
There was no one there and I felt to blame
I felt like my world was coming to an end
It was as if I'd lost my best friend
I walked away with my head hanging down
Trying to look pleasant
Trying to hide my frown
My mind started wondering and I couldn't stop
The more I stepped the more tears dropped
I tried to control it, but couldn't hide the pain
Each tear hit the ground as if it were rain
The faster I stepped the louder I cried
That's when I realized, with you
A part of me died too

My Son Tyrik

My sweet little baby, Tyrik
You came into this world,
Your lungs were too weak
The pain I feel, I can't explain
I'm thankful that I held you
For that I can't complain
Each night when I close my eyes
A vision of you I'll see
The very thought is comforting
That you are a part of me
Even though our time here was short
We shall meet again
When I arrive at Heaven's Gate
I pray that you let me in.

Daddy

When you died,
I lost all words
Couldn't think of anything to say
Daddy
When you died
It took a while before I cried
I had so much to do
Daddy
I wish there was just a moment
A second that I could have seen you
Daddy
When you died
I wanted to scream
I wanted to shout
I wanted to pull all of my hair out
Then I realized if I did all of that
It wouldn't bring you back
Daddy
So here I am
Taking each day as if it were my last
Remembering the good times
And the bad times with each year that pass
Because at the end of the day
The Lord had His way
And called you home to Glory
Daddy
I will always carry this love
And it's not the end of our story
That day will come

And I'll pay my fare
To ride that train up there
On that day
I'll have those words to say
No matter the time
No matter the place
My heart still feels the same
I love you forever and ever
Because you are my Daddy

My Grandpa

Grandpa wore coveralls
And smoked Prince Albert in the can
Grandpa was tall in stature but a gentleman
Grandpa left us far too soon in my book
But trying to live without Grandma seemed to be all it took
Grandpa left us quietly just asleep in the bed
But Grandpa didn't leave without me there just beneath his head
You see Grandpa meant the world to me
His death created a lot of pain
Grandpa I promise one day we'll meet again
Until that day please continue to watch over us
Even though you know at times things can get rough
That's when I think you're there the most
Grandpa was a country man that worked the fields
And sat under a shade tree
The way I liked it
Just my Grandpa and me

Uncle

My heart stopped and my body began to shake
The thought of losing you was more than I could take
The rambling of my thoughts was like an earth quake
How did this happen?
How did we get here?
Did they really just call me to tell me death for my
uncle was near?
Then I thought about the last time we spoke
How I laughed and you joked
I just wanted to get there to be by your side
I didn't expect to be across the hall the morning you
died.
These days have been hard for me because I loved
you so much
I'm just glad that we always stayed in touch
The only comfort I have is that you're at peace now
I can't lie though; I'm still trying to figure out how.
How did this happen?
You just had a birthday.
No one imagined you would leave us this way.
The night time is the hardest, I can't sleep.
I lay there in darkest and weep.
I realize it will get a little better with time,
But right now, that doesn't ease my mind.
We all miss you so much, it's hard to accept.
We all love you dearly.
As quiet as it's kept,
I knew you were leaving that night as you slept.

LIFE

Emptiness

Emptiness, Loneliness
Dying to be free
Those were the feelings
Feelings that were a part of me
As I woke up from that pain
I began to live again
Love, Happiness, Joy and Peace
Is what I have replaced all the sadness with
I realized it was there all along
I had to find the strength and the power to carry on
So to those hurtful feelings of yesterday
I have one thing to say
You may have had space in my head
But no more
I have a new outlook on life
I won't feel emptiness again
I know my worth, I'm loving who I am
Will I no longer feel pain?
Why, yes, of course
But, I realize now
I have a choice to make
I can wallow in my pain
And leave the emptiness inside
Or I can stand tall and
Deal with it without foolish pride
My good days have come and gone
I'm heading for the great ones
So, sit back and watch me while I get it done.

Acceptance

Accept me for me, like I accept you
Is that too much for you to do?
I understand sometimes I can make it hard
But at all times I'm on guard
Guard from things that could bring me down
Guard from things that turn me all around
I'm only human so I can make mistakes
Accept me for me, that's all it takes
I have no one that could ever understand
What it's like to need a helping hand
A hand during bad times, there's only a few
Do you feel as though that hand could be you?
Sometimes I'm silly and play silly games, but that's
how it goes
I need a friend and that's how it shows
Don't shut me out in my hour of need
I'm like a caged animal that needs to be freed
Freed from pressures that weighs on my mind
Freed from this world which is so unkind
Freed from every problem you could dream about
So if you want to be a friend, then a friend you be
But do me a favor friend, please set me free

Untitled

Life,
One big puzzle one big mess
Filled with pain, rarely happiness
When you look, one never finds
A place of freedom, somewhere divine
Where colors are many and prejudice are few
Somewhere to go so you can be you
If I had the power
I'd build such a place
Full of hope and full of grace
That would be the place to be
So you could be you, and I could be me

Just a Seat

I want a seat at the table
A chance to show that I'm able
Able to engage in deep conversation
Because I have the power of persuasion
To bring anyone up to speed on my ideas
Whether they agree or disagree
There should be a seat at the table for me

I want a seat at the table
To showcase who I am in all my glory
To sit down with the elite and tell my story
To bring to the attention of those that have forgotten
The real reason behind the things they've all gotten
You see, before me there were others sitting in that chair
That's why I'm so honored and trying to get there

I want a seat at the table
No, I demand a seat at the table
There's none other qualified than I
I want a seat at the table, instead of idly standing by

Time to Remember

Looking out my window sill
Everything is quiet, everything is still
I remember climbing trees
Riding bikes and skinning up my knees
I remember having a safe place to run
Always playing games and having fun
I remember roller skating down the street
Gathering on the corner where we all would meet
Taking off the skates to play jump rope
Double Dutch was the best and boy was I dope
Jumping on one leg and criss cross
That was the best
Seeing who could jump the fastest contest
   RED HOT PEPPERS
Boy, did I have fun as a kid
I can't remember everything that I did
But I do know that today
Life isn't so fun anymore
All of the games that I played
Left a lot of scars that stayed
Sometimes pain is just a part of life
But it doesn't mean it doesn't cut sharp like a knife
Heartache is no fun
There's no fun games to play, no safe place to run
You just have to stand there and wait for it to pass
The trophy goes to the one that's standing last
Getting older ain't no joke
Having responsibilities like paying bills
Trying to keep from going broke

Providing for the family, not many friends
Making sure ends are meeting and meetings end
No time for red light green light or Simon says
No Mother May I, because Pop went that weasel
And Jack jumped out that box
Now it's all about the School of Hard Knocks
Getting older means the games were supposed to
stop
All of the silliness and playfulness just drops
It's time to stand up straight
Put on that suit
Get on that job and make that bread
All of those fun memories out of your head
Now it's all about that paper chase
Sometimes forgetting to say grace
When you sit down to grab a bite to eat
Because it's something quick faster than a heart beat
Always on the grind
Never taking the time
To remember
Remember how Daddy used to take us apple picking
How if we cut up, he's give us both a whipping
Remember how Grandma's kitchen used to smell
Thinking if you didn't go to church you'd burn in hell
Remember how there's more to life
Than just making a living
There's love, hope, and giving
Giving back to those that paved the way
So we could have this day to remember
Remember how we used to walk outside in bare feet
Making mud pies and the dirt we'd eat

Running around without a care in the world
Boys being boys and girls being girls
Grandma's house was the perfect place
Beating all my cousins in a relay race
I'm glad I finally took the time to remember
Reflecting on the past is not a bad thing
Sometimes you just have to let freedom ring
Getting down and depressed is not the way to get
about life
Don't stay focused on the heartache and strife
Just take a few minutes a day
To get in touch with the kid inside
And take the time to remember

Good Love

Are you sure you're just a friend to me?
Because you see
You give good love
Not that physical love
But that f*$% your mind love
And
Make you wish for more
Because you've never had it like this before
You know that feeling of after glow
When the whole world knows
That
You've
Just
Made love
My walk is different
My speech is different
I have that certain glow
It's because of you, my friend
And I hope the feeling never ends
Because you give good love
Not that physical love
But that F$%^ your mind love
You're such a good friend to me
I'm enjoying this ever so greatly
We have that chemistry
That level of intimacy
I will follow wherever you lead
This is so powerful
We're like Wonder Twins

I'm so glad that we're friends
But if you ever decide to take it to that level
Baby you give good love
It could be that physical kind
Where our bodies are entwined
And we do that dance between the sheets
And I can lay there in silence listening to our hearts beat
Because baby you give good love
But then again
You are my friend
And I would never wanna take the chance
On a romance
And jeopardize what we have now
You see
Sometimes the chemistry
And intimacy
Can fade away in a relationship
I don't want to lose what we have now
Over a few hours or a few years
Because baby you give good love
I would take the risk
If there were a guarantee
That we could be for eternity
Because baby, you give good love

Be

I wish I could be
That fearless 17-year-old that took the world by storm
That 19-year-old that made them fearful and stood out
from the norm
I wish I could be
That 22-year-old that stood her ground and never
looked back at her mistakes
That 25-year-old that handled her business no matter
what it would take
I wish I could be
That 30-year-old that raised her son to be respectful
of others
That proud black lady that hung out with other single
mothers
I wish I could be
That 40-year-old that wakes up and is thankful for the
bruises
Instead of the frightened little thing that everyone
abuses
I wish I could be fearless like a lion
Kind like a kitten
Mean like a junk yard dog
I wish I could be
Me
But tell me, who is that exactly?

My Sun Rise

My sun rise is in your eyes
And the thunder is your voice
My happiness is somewhere
I pretend I have a choice
You see
I smile every day
No matter what the weather's going to be
You see
My smile hides my pain and my history
Tomorrow is not promised so I live for today
But what does it even matter

My sun rise is in your eyes
And I must learn to see
Sunrise being in your eyes is not helping me
That day will come
When your light will dim
So what good is that to me
I need my own sunrise in my eyes
So that I can be free

Beautiful

Was it the color of my skin
That made your bones shake within?
Was it the sight of my size
That made you so surprised?
Did the look on my face
Make you lower your pace?
Could it have been the deepness of my glare
That caused such a stare?
Was it the confidence in my stand and the pride in my
walk,
That made you too afraid to talk?
For if it were, you certainly are not alone
There are so many others like you just a society
clone.
I fear no one as ignorant as you
I feel for anyone that do.
When I look in the mirror, I look with grace
And say, "Thank you Jesus for this beautiful black
face."

Unchained

That saying, "that's off the chain"
Is exactly how I'm feeling right now
Being unchained to the negativity
The social media hype is destroying us
Destroying the peace, order and trust
There is no more sacred privacy
Everything is created for the world to see
Unchained realities lost in translation
Hiding from real life and physical relation
Living behind computer screens and keyboards
Taking dictation and direction from android
Lifestyle changes and personality disorders
Have created such a strain
People suppressing emotions hiding pain
Creating falsehoods in their mental fantasy
Avoiding physical contact and reality
Focused on the impossible
Constantly becoming unchained
Trapped within the social media haze
Caught up in the drama filled maze
Sharing snap chats of their life for a like
While the suicide rate continues to spike
Unchained
That reality created in the mind
Slowly sinking further behind

Alone

I stand alone as one soul
Quickly falling into a hole
I run and run to get away
But the beast is not going astray
Where can I run?
Where can I hide?
There's no place for it's all inside
My eyes see darkness and my heart feels pain
Together they give me such a strain
Soon pain will overcome darkness and then what a
mess
I can no longer be strong, I must give in I guess
I'm reaching, reaching for a helping hand
Somebody, anybody, please understand
When the wind blows tonight, I'm going to disappear
Disappear into the twilight
I stand alone as one soul
Quickly, quickly, quickly falling into a hole

Mizz Understood No More

I went from Mizz Understood to MecheleFlows
Because now a sistah knows
Just how the game goes and all the key players
After so many years,
Shedding a few tears I finally realize
It takes more than a few harsh words and a few lies
To break me.
Now I stand here
My mind is clear on what it is I'm here to do
I came to reclaim my power
Uplift the people and try to educate you too
Don't ever allow your voices to fall silent
It's a sign of weakness
Often people take advantage of a person's meekness
Never realizing that meekness does not equate push
over
While they are pushing it's only lifting you higher
Like the Phoenix rises and sets itself on fire
Out of the ashes comes a new creature
Stronger than ever before
That's why I'm MecheleFlows
Not Mizz Understood anymore

Party

Make the party jump
Make the party jump
Get up on the dance floor
And let's tear the club up

It's Friday and I'm ready to have some fun
Call up my girls to see who's down to run
Got the fly gear on and I'm ready to be seen
Getting the do right, you know what I mean.

Make the party jump
Make the party jump
Get up on the floor
And let's tear this club up

All up in the place
About to hit the floor
The beat is bangin'
Couldn't ask for much more
The DJ is setting the room on fire
The beat is so hot its taking us higher

Party up and moving to the beat
Met a fly guy on the floor
Feeling his heat

DJ keep doing your thing
The party is jumping

Baby Boy

My baby boy
Oh how I remember carrying you
Even though I was only twenty-two
Your dad and I got prepared
I can't lie, we were scared.
We could barely afford to pay attention
We didn't have much money
Or a lot of things I won't mention
I didn't know about bringing a life into this world
Not to mention we thought you were a girl
We both wanted a girl
Why? I have no idea
I'm happy to say, you being a boy was a surprise
Yet again, we didn't realize
Having a son was the best fit for us

My baby boy
Has grown into a young man
I'm sitting back watching
Cheering, being your number one fan
Through all the road blocks in your way
And all of the negative things the teachers would say
Look at you now, out here on your own
Working, living and being all grown
I couldn't be any prouder
Nor could I shout any louder
My baby boy is a grown man now

LOVE

Crush

 Would you look at me differently if you knew how I felt?
How when you walk in the room my whole-body melts.
Would you continue to be a friend to me or would it scare you off?
You see,
I've been battling these feelings so long
Trying to hold them back; trying to be strong
But there's something about you
That makes me want to be with you.
It's hard to explain with just words on a page
It's hard to express from a mic and a stage
I'm afraid to tell you how I feel
Afraid it will make the fantasy real
You see, in my mind we're a pair
Doing things together, going here, going there.
But in the real world I am just your friend
That's where it all started; I guess that's where it will end.
Maybe one day the feelings fade away.
I see you as just a friend
That way I won't have to worry about, what is fake and what is real
Because I will no longer hide how I feel
I will accept you for the friend you are to me
I will know in my heart
A friend is all you'll ever be

The Vows

I remember the day we stood side by side
You were the groom and I was your bride
We recited the words as we were instructed to do
Our greatest moment and expression of I love you
We kissed one another to seal the deal
That very moment the words became real
I accepted you in sickness and health
I accepted you whether broke or in wealth
We promised each other a lifetime
Of me being yours and you being mine
Even though we were standing there a nervous wreck
we took a vow
To stay together but look at us now
Things got off track somehow
We're both coming in and out barely saying a word
You're caught up in your own little world
Somehow time has passed and we've lost our
connection
Bit by bit we're no longer showing affection
Unfortunately, this marriage is headed in the wrong
direction
Even though neither one of us wanted to face the
facts
Our love train had quickly jumped the tracks
At least we both agreed we will do what's best for us
Because truthfully there is no marriage without trust
Fast forward to the day we met again
And the judge agreed and brought the vows to an end

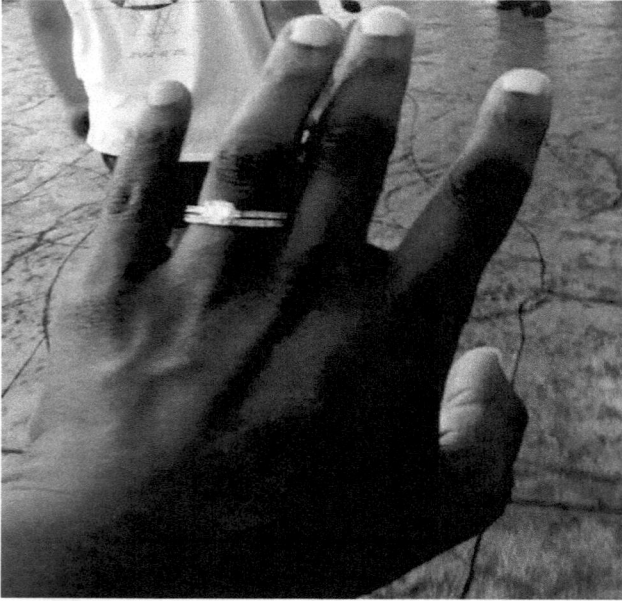

Thoughts of You

There's not a day that I don't think of you
I involve you in everything I do
In the morning and during the late night
I find myself wishing you were here holding me tight
I can see your face when I close my eyes
I'm so in love, but to my surprise
It's been so long and we're still apart
Only by bodies never by our heart
This experience has taught me well
Being away from you is pure hell
I hold my head up high and reach deep inside
And there's all the feelings I try to hide
When I get home I promise they'll show
I just can't wait to let you know

I Miss You

I never thought I would but baby I do
I realize now how much I miss you
Every minute of the day I can say
You're on my mind in a crazy way
I miss your gentle touch and soft kiss
Then too, the tone of your voice I miss
I need to hear you call my name
Baby without you I'm not the same
You bring out all the joy in me
Wrapped in your arms is the place to be
I miss your smile and your handsome face
I just miss your presence around this place
Please come back as soon as you can
Never to let you go again is my plan

I Used 2 Love U

Tall, Handsome and a smile all a glow
That's nothing compared to his ego
Charismatic
Attractive
And such a delight
Until he gets you alone at night
Those eyes so sweet
When he speaks
Ooooh, your knees go weak
Who is this northern charmer that all the ladies go
crazy for?
He's not the average dude next door
He had a profound effect on me
Love had me so blind that I could not see
Even though I gave my all to him
He gave his to Tanya, Lisa, and Kim
It took a while to figure that out
Boy, did I yell and he did shout
He tried to convince me it was all in my mind
But ladies, love ain't that blind
So, when he came by to tell me, I knew
I cut him off by saying, "I know, and I used to love
you"

Untitled

As I stare from my window so high
I can see happiness but still I cry
I cry tears but tears of joy no pain
For in such a short time there love I've gained
Never before feelings so strong
A love like this could never be wrong
As the tears drop I start to smile
A pleasant face walks down the isle
A smile so bright it matches the sun
I can say I'm the lucky one
Lucky in love to be so true
There's no reason at all for feeling blue
As he approaches I start to smile, what else to do
Except whisper the words I LOVE YOU

Infatuation

I'm in love
I smile every time I see him
A feeling comes over me that I can't explain
Just recently learned his name
Now I'm dying to spit game
In his direction
To be the object of his affection
In my book he's the picture of perfection
With his chocolate brown complexion
I realize that we just met
But something about him feels right
I never ever believed in love at first sight
However, now at this particular moment I do
Because I'm all caught up in his Voodoo
I would love to wrap my arms around his neck and
lean in for a kiss
Most likely standing on my tip toes coz his height I
can't miss
The brightness of his smile just captivates me
Those lips melt me down and no one else can see
Today I watched him walk down the street
I was checking him from his head to his feet
I have his walk memorized
His swag, his confidence had me hypnotized
Slowly I turned my head to follow as he moved up the
street
I held my breath and could hear my heart beat
I know he saw me staring but that's alright
I had him locked within my sight

I slowly parted my lips as if to speak
But I waved my hand instead
All sorts of corny things was coming to my mind
He's not the type of brother you hit with a corny line
I'm not sure if he's even interested in me
I guess time will tell I just have to wait and see
Tonight my prayer is "Lord if this man is for me and
you decide we should speak.
Please God let it be next week."

Old Flame

I never thought I would see him again
I always considered him a good friend
Of course we were a little deeper than that
But I'm not saying I want that old thing back
It appeared the stars never could align
For me to be his and he to be mine
If I could have anything it would be new game
The opportunity to get to see if he's at all the same
I have memories and that's fine
Memories of us on the dance floor dancing to R
Kelly's *"Bump n' Grind"*
I can't help but wonder have things gotten better with
age
You know like reached a higher stage
I do have memories of the past, so it wouldn't be hard
to gage
But hold up, hold up
I failed to look
Did he have a relationship status posted on
Facebook?
I'm so excited to be reunited that I never thought to
ask
I'm not trying to have a chic trying to kick my a$$
But for now I will enjoy the reconnect with an old
friend
Leaving all the pages open to discover how the story
ends
I'm not going to pretend
This is a very special friend

Our first chapter was written without an end
So if he's available
And interested to see
I would be game, but only if he's free
I don't have time for drama coming at me.
Who knows, maybe that flame is now dim
There may not be anything there for me or him

Untitled

For the longest time
I thought it was just sex for me.
I loved how you touched my body.
Then that day, you spoke to my heart.
I should have known it was real from the start.
You have this way of making me smile
I would climb every mountain and walk every mile.
Just to be with you because I see
That you bring out the best in me.
Even though I try to fight it,
I have to admit
Without you in my life,
My life ain't shit
Sure I can conquer these battles
Bringing home the awards
But you by my side is the greatest reward
I love you baby, from the depths of my soul.
I want to be with you until we grow old.
When we cannot speak anymore
With wrinkles so deep
I want to lay there beside you in eternal sleep.

The End

If this is the end
I say let it be
'cause you've given
The best to me
Over the years
We've had a time
But in my heart
You will always be mine
If this is the end
I'll take it all in stride
I refuse to hide
Behind my foolish pride
I'll say it now
Like I said it before
I love you forever more

Kind of Love

I want that Michelle and Barack Obama kind of love
That fist bump because we got this kind of love
I want that pillow fight in the middle of the night
Just because kind of love
That we can talk without speaking kind of love
I want that late-night love making like we have
nowhere to be kind of love
I want that Mia and Lance kind of love
That he call out and I all out of work kind of love
That late-night movie on the sofa like teenager's kind
of love
But really
Who am I kidding?
I want that Godly love
That we pray together to stay together kind of love
I want that when he's weak I'm strong kind of love
That we down for each other in any kind of weather
kind of love
I want that
He's my guiding light even though we may fuss and
fight kind of love
That
He snores and I hate doing chores but we're good
kind of love
That I wear a bonnet and PJ's at night while he stays
up late watching the game
Kind of love
I want that

He leaves the cap off the toothpaste and never cleans the tub
But that's ok because I love him anyway kind of love
Knowing all of this just makes me wish
 But I will wait for that special love
Because I deserve it

Stronghold

We were like two magnets
The attraction was strong
Never taking the time to consider
Who's right or who's wrong
I was caught up in the waterfall
As the evidence of our love broke down my walls
The barriers were released and the river flowed
Taking it all in and the feelings showed
We were lost on that river in our raft
Caught up in one another; perfecting our craft
Crashing against the rocks
We navigated through the rough seas
Current so strong and we doing as we please
Experiencing that ultimate connection
Expressing our mutual affection
Releasing the showers of joy through our exhalation
Because we reached our final destination

As We Lay

I sit here with a grin because I'm pleased
Even though I feel weak in the knees
I stretch out my leg and let out a sigh
As I place my leg between your thigh
The love you give makes me scream
I can't explain the way that I cream
Your kiss is soft and gentle on my lips
I love the way your hands massage my hips
You turn my body into a sex machine
Steadily pumpin overtime, if you know what I mean
Your love is the object of my desire
Your lips, your hands, your tongue ignite my fire
As I lay here in a state of satisfaction
I notice you look surprised by my reaction
Love is like a river that flows so long
Making love is an emotion that is extremely strong
That feeling that two people share
Is oh so precious and oh so rare
When you see the joy love can bring
You will find it is the most wonderful thing
As I lay here my body feels light
I close my eyes and enjoy my delight
For tonight my dear has been nothing but joy
Joy experienced between a girl and a boy
Good night my love I can say no more
My eyes are closing as I begin to snore
I take with me thoughts of your love
The love we just made is what I'll dream of

Come Back

As the rain falls, so are my tears.
The thought of losing you is my greatest fear.
We've had our ups and down
That's no reason to give up now
Baby, can't we start over again
Forever about the who, what, where and when
Baby, can't you see my heart is aching?
Can't you see my heart is breaking?
Tears are falling down my face.
There's no love in this place.
We have to make it right.
Please let's not fight.
I want you in my life.
The walls are closing in
There's no room to breathe
It's unbelievable that you can't see
What you have done to me
I gave you my all but it was not enough
I have no idea
How much clearer I can be
Expressing how I feel
I'm standing here waiting, praying this isn't real
Baby, can't you come back to me
My love is waiting unconditionally
My heart is open, my arms are waiting
Baby, can't you come back to me?

<u>When</u>

Love is when
        You see their face everywhere you look
        When a simple smile was all it took
        When the hottest of summer
        Or coldest of winter you want them near
        To hold your body and soul so dear
        During the rainy days and cloudy nights
        Only their arms can hold you right

Love is when
        You put their heart and needs before your own
        When they decide to leave you all alone
        When you pick up the pieces and carry on
        When you take with you that love and kindness
        And would never do something foolish

Love is when
        The relationship comes to a peaceful end
        And you find yourselves the best of friends

New Beginnings

You say I don't understand you
You have given it your last try
I'm going to accept that
Not ask you your reasons why
For years we have struggled
To find a common ground
For years we keep finding ourselves on this merry go
round
Constantly traveling in circles
Never once stopping to see
We were both on the same ride
But we sat separately
You were facing one way and I was not looking back
Neither one of us made an effort to keep this love on
track
So now that we've said good-bye
It doesn't mean everything will end
Once we get past the hurt feelings, a new friendship
can begin

How Can I

How can I tell you that my love is true?
When you keep acting the way you do
One minute you want me, the next you don't
One minute you make love to me, the next you won't
How can I share my life with you?
When you keep acting the way you do
One minute you're there right by my side
The next you're running off to hide
One minute you're telling me you want me near
The next you're acting out of fear
How can I trust you when you keep acting the way
you do?
One minute you're sharing and holding me tight
The next you're not coming home at night
One minute you're telling me you're with friends
The next you're forgetting the who, where and when's
How can I share my inner thoughts with you?
When you keep acting the way you do
One minute you're listening with such care
The next you're wishing you're not even there
One minute you're telling me how to react
The next you're carrying on like your answers are fact
How can I continue to love you?
When you keep acting the way that you do.

Bitter Sweet

Special memories are all that we share
You've got your family and they need you there
There's no way for me to try to compare
Because I know the feelings we share
Even though several years have gone by
The connection is still present between you and I
The only difference is our lives have changed
The fantasy of there being an us was fun
But at the end of the day we're fooling no one
You will never leave and I would never ask you to
Just know that I will always love you.

It was so special that our paths crossed again
It felt so good to reminisce with an old friend
We know that the past has to stay in the past
Things are so different now
There are so many factors to consider
I guess that's when the sweet turns bitter.

About the Author

Michelle L. Sutton is a native of Boston, Massachusetts currently living in the metro Atlanta, Georgia area. Poetry has always been her passion. She has been writing poetry since she was a child. Some of her influences are Zora Neale Hurston, Langston Hughes, Nikki Giovanni and Maya Angelou.

Over the years, Michelle entered various poetry contests and wrote poems for special occasions. That prompted her to start a home based greeting card business. Michelle is the former owner and operator of World of Writing (WoW) Publications whereas she created greeting cards, announcements and poems for special occasions. She is a poet and spoken word artist. Michelle goes by the stage name of MecheleFlows. She has performed in venues in the local Atlanta area. Michelle entered and won several poetry contests over the years, which resulted in her works being published in anthologies.

Michelle is an U.S. Army veteran currently employed as a paralegal specialist.

You can follow her on Facebook, YouTube and Instagram @mecheleflows.

www.ingramcontent.com/pod-product-compliance
Lightning Source LLC
Chambersburg PA
CBHW060609030426
42337CB00018B/3015